D1387838

CONTENTS

The Fireside Book

A picture and a poem for every mood
chosen by

David Hope

Printed and published by D.C. THOMSON & CO., LTD.,
185 Fleet Street, LONDON EC4A 2HS. © D.C. Thomson & Co., Ltd., 2007

FEBRUARY WREN

WHY so now,
so bold in fleeting snow,
mercurial mite,
wee passerine,
neat, nimble, oh-so-clean
careening troglodyte?

From tub to tub,
harvesting insect and grub
you go.
Even as I brazenly stare
you seem not to care.
How so?

Another day
you'd quickly flit away.
Yet now you dash
from stick to budding stick
tic-tic, tic-tic,
so suddenly brash.

Has this cold snap
curbed your warning stirrrup?
Will your shy habit
reappear
once warmer days are here
and Spring's afoot?

John Ellis

PRIMROSES

AMONGST high rocks
I love to see
a glory of pale primroses.

Earthbound, I plunder market stalls,
buy more cultivated plants, bury
my face in their sweet honey.

I shoehorn my shy flowers
into tubs and urns, place them
askew in a broken old kettle

set amongst shells and driftwood.
sea haar nips my arms as I toil,
firming up soil, sprinkling water,

gives urgency to my work now,
welcoming in
the first frail bouquet of Spring.

Ruth Walker

MY LITTLE FRIEND

WHEN I take out my rake and hoe,
My little friend just seems to know,
Some tasty morsels I'll provide
As soon as I start work outside.
He watches me without a sound,
Perched on my spade stuck in the ground,
Small wonder that our spirits soar,
Such is our simple sweet rapport.
With red bib shining in the sun,
A special magic spell is spun,
We work together side by side,
From morning till the eventide.
No truer friendship could be stirred,
Than this between a man and bird.

Brian H. Gent

SEQUEL

THE day's rescued, redeemed,
the snow is all but gone.
For a brief while it seemed
Winter had proclaimed
Spring adjunct to its season

But this late March afternoon
has come with a warm brush,
sweeping pathway, lawn,
and all the borders clean
of smothering snow and slush.

Now, blackbird and thrush
twitter again and trill,
and through the quick thaw push
the most cheerful cache
of primroses and daffodil.

And down the ivied aisle,
where melting snow still drips,
the long-legged, genial
gardener, bright Sol,
in yellow slippers trips.

John Ellis

AWAKENING

EARLY morn, and dawn is breaking,
  Waking sleepers from their dreams,
Sending fragile sunlight creeping,
Dappling grass in golden gleams.
Dew is on the field and hedgerows,
Blossom hangs as fine as lace,
Gentle is the lambs' soft bleating,
Greeting daybreak's shining face.
In the cottage, life is stirring,
Lamps are lit, a kettle sings.
Outside in the starry meadows,
Spring waits breathless in the wings.

Margaret Ingall

RIVER OF LIFE

LIFE is a river and steadily flowing,
  Catching the sunlight, sparkling and glowing,
Over the rocks and the pebbles and ridges,
Under the willow trees, under the bridges.
On through the darkness, the bright stars reflecting,
Meeting the little streams, joining, connecting,
Deep pools and silent pools, water cascading,
Hearing the wind and the birds serenading.
On to the ocean, now gently and slowing,
A distant horizon, a place of unknowing.
The river of life, flowing strong, flowing free,
Into Eternity, out to the sea.

Iris Hesselden

SPRING

THE month of March has come at last,
The worst of Winter now has passed,
But, until it's really Spring,
March will have her final fling.

Rain must fall and winds must blow
Before we sharpen spade and hoe;
Nature needs no hand of man
To help her with her future plan.

Snowdrops bloom in wood and field,
Chill winds never made them yield,
Crocuses in drifts close by
Turn coloured faces to the sky.

Gorse and heather on the moor,
No wonder that our spirits soar,
To see their colourful display
Overcomes the dullest day.

Willows show a hint of green,
Waters still reflect the sheen;
So many signs to bring us cheer,
Now that another Spring is near.

Brian H. Gent

MARCH LIGHT

TODAY, a beam of light
(So pure, aspic white)
Streamed
Into the living room,
And screamed,
"Spring has come."
Nothing had changed,
Only the hands
Of the seasons' clock
Slowly ticking off
The darkened corners,
And turning Winter's night
Into the flickering light
Of Spring.

David Elder

TEAPOTS LINE
YOUR STAIRS

SQUIRRELLED in each corner,
leaving little room to tread,
plain and small, grandiose and tall,
your teapots stand on guard.

At every step each one seems
to pour out a little more of you,
and recommend your chosen blend
of motley shapes, a curious brew.

Junk shop, gift shop, auction room,
all feature in your ceramic affairs.
Recherché, bright, a sheer delight,
these teapots that line your stairs.

John Ellis

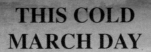

THIS COLD
MARCH DAY

THEY'RE wearing their blankets
  This cold March day,
Waiting for children;
Nibbling hours away.
Beauty black, and brown,
And here's a dapple grey
Nodding near a five-barred gate,
This cold March day.

A pale pond with a gaggle
Atop its muddy banks,
Hankering for bread,
Honking grateful thanks,
And here's a mother goose,
Downy, white and grey,
Settling to warm her eggs
This cold March day.

Don Robinson

BURIED TREASURE

YOU don't need a desert island
   Where palm trees gently sway,
With fearsome eye-patched pirates
Anchored in the bay,
No need for crinkled parchment map
And "X" to mark the spot,
Nor clever coded messages
To add spice to the plot,
The treasure that is hidden
Is there for all to find,
And is packed with precious jewels
Of each and every kind,
There is pure gold and ivory
And gems of azure blue,
Beyond the dreams of avarice
In wondrous tint and hue,
So I'll tell you the secret,
No need for pick or spade,
For it is simply waiting there
In every leafy glade,
You'll be rich beyond compare,
Good fortune's praises sing,
The treasure trove will be revealed
When flowers bloom next Spring!

Brian H. Gent

GRASSLAND

THERE are no flat fields here;
each slope rises and tilts
beyond the limits of hedge and dyke.

From the high knowes,
where granite muscles through stretched soil
and leafy rye grass withers first in the sun,
waves of timothy dip and fall
to marshy hollows sprouting reed and sedge.

Lost between contours
tussocks of cocksfoot and clover,
yellow clusters of ragwort;
at the edges sit nettle and whin.

Across fresh acres the eager-mouthed herd
pull on new blades of meadow fescue;
leave cloven rain cups radiating from gateways:
the fingerprints of pasture.

Jim Carruth

MARCH HARES

THEY stand in the middle
 Of the green field,
Sniffing their madness,
Contemplating the world
And this game
Of rounders
They think they're in.

Suddenly they're off,
Dashing about,
At full speed,
Trying to make
The next base,
And beat the imaginary ball
That will have them out.

David Elder

IONA FERRY

IT'S the smell I remember —
  The dizziness of diesel, tarry rope, wood sheened like toffee.
The sea was waving in the wind, a dancing;
I wanted it to be rough and yet I didn't.
My mother and I snugged under the awning,
To a dark rocking. We were as low as the waves,
All of us packed in tight like bales of wool.
The engine roared alive; its tremor
Juddered through the wood and thrilled me, beat my heart;
The shore began fading behind the white curl of our hum.
Fourteen days lay barefoot on the island —
Still asleep, their eyes all shut,
And yet I knew them all already,
Felt them in my pocket like polished stones —
Their orchids, their hurt-white sand, their larksong.
At last the engine dropped and died —
We bumped in backwards to the jetty
Climbed aboard the island.

Kenneth C. Steven

COUNTRY WOMAN

YOU saw her with apple cheeks and woolly hat,
    wheeling home whole branches in an old pram
to be cut into logs on her saw horse.

Or she would be rotovating her ground.
She had a way with plants and animals:
her bee hives produced gallons of honey.

For each child in the Sunday School,
she made a bag for gathering acorns.
She crocheted hats from recycled plastic,

cut carpet squares for the cold Church Hall chairs.
Up and down the hill she went, to the Kirk
and to the bowls. Someone there once asked her,

"Would there be a bowling green in Heaven?"
"I'll check with the minister," she replied.
Celestial swards were surely there, he assured her,
but be prepared to play in a match next Thursday!

Ruth Walker

LOVE IN A MIST

BEHIND the wall
Of my city garden
She came to me
Late in the Spring,
Dressed in the bright blue
Of a perfect
Provençale sky.

Always reliable,
And so discreet
My love in a mist,
When we met at dusk
In our secret
Rendez-vous border
Hidden from the wind.

But after the harvest moon faded,
It all fell apart:
She cried her petals
To the ground,
He face hardened,
And her head became
A crown of spikes.

My love in a mist
Had become
The devil in a bush.

David Elder

TRANQUILLITY

BLUE the sky above the river.
   Green the rushes and the reeds.
White the swans, serenely gliding,
Brown the path which tempts and leads.
Summer colours, gently healing,
Soothing heart and mind and soul.
Take us onward through the seasons
Though the Winter tempests roll.

Purple on the distant mountains,
Scents of Autumn in the air,
Keep and store these peaceful moments
When the days are less than fair.
Seek and find an inner courage
Ere the troubled times begin,
See a smoother path before you,
Find tranquillity within.

Iris Hesselden

WHISPERS IN THE DARK

So, at last, the sun has set,
All is still and quiet, yet,
There, in between the conifers,
In lanes and hedges something stirs.
Gentle whisping murmurings,
Send bats and owls on silent wings,
Into the blackness of the night,
On their secret mystic flight.
Badgers snuffle in the wood,
Where glow-worms hawthorn bushes flood.
Moles and hedgehogs wake from sleep
And into mossy pathways creep.
So little creatures leave their mark,
When nature whispers in the dark.

Brian H. Gent

PAINT A POEM

PAINT a poem, blue and red.
Let poppies bleed on a canvas bed
and bluebells shed oily tears.

Wash your brushes in the sea,
then let them drip
on purple lakes.
Paint with crimson flakes
from a setting sun,
and sweep your shadows boldly.

Splatter words like drops of rain,
and soak the woollen grain
with whispers of ochre.

Paint in Autumn's mood.
Expose, compose, unfold
its leafy glades and mellow shades
in words of light and beauty.

Paint your words on distant skies,
and frame the poem
with your eyes.

Mo Crawshaw

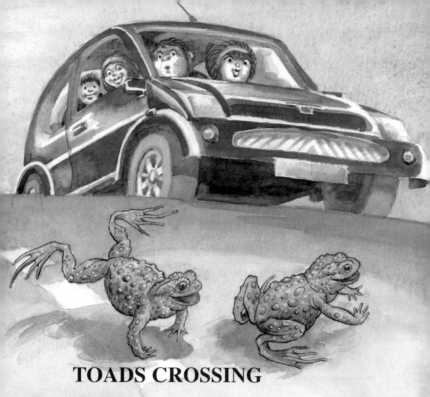

TOADS CROSSING

MIGRATION time, and the common toad
risks life and limb to cross the road.
In droves, by hundreds, one and all,
answering some primeval call,
they travel light, they travel late,
to pastures new to procreate.

But if some thoughtful resident,
of kindness and without payment,
had not erected this bold plea:
TOADS CROSSING, PLEASE DRIVE CAREFULLY!
then every season, more and more,
they would diminish by the score.

So watch out for these pilgrim toads,
and please don't race down country roads.

John Ellis

RAPTURE

I HAVE a memory of youth
  that pierces me on Summer days
when skies are tall and scoured smooth,
enamelled with an azure glaze.
Walking through a country field,
Captive to the clover's scent,
I sang to blackbirds, ill-concealed,
Embellishing a farmer's fence.
With plumage gleaming purple-black,
And long and slender glossy beaks,
They plumped their breasts, then arched
their backs
And raised a canticle to me.
Oh! A trusting child at play
caught a glimpse of Heaven's spires,
and worshipped on that sweetest day
with a winged and feathered choir.

Rachel Wallace-Oberle

CAT IN CLOVER

A MINI-TIGER stalks the Summer grass
   Where clover nestles close to daisy flowers.
Languidly pacing on his stately way,
He plans to while away the golden hours.

Yet quite nearby this green and grassy plot
A flourishing of tempting catmint grows.
A verdant ear is twitched, a soft paw lifts,
The scent of catmint titillates his nose.

No longer just a laid back garden cat,
But one with every sense on red alert.
Our pie-eyed puss-cat rolls upon his back
And casts his dignity among the dirt.

A cat possessed by catmint is a sight
Prone to make passing humans double over.
Yet any puss thus fragrantly indulged
Is certain to become a cat in clover.

Joan Howes

COUNTRY CHURCH

WIND rattles the oak door,
    begging to be let in.
Branches tap tall window panes,

letting leaves caress the glass.
Inside, deep silence
holds the small histories

of forgotten things.
An umbrella, left behind
because the sun came out,

a Fair Isle beret worked in red and green
abandoned now since Christmas time.
In the vestibule, a pewter plate

that once embraced florins, half crowns
and threepenny bits.
Then, within, the rows of empty pews,

as sunlight fades the crimson carpet.
A butterfly, with outstretched wings,
basks in the warmth.

There is a lingering perfume
of full-blown flowers.
The wall-mounted Cross with empty halo

casts its shadow upon the Communion Table.
Outside, a choir of insects hum and dance,
a flock of sheep crop the grass
and lazy cows ruminate.

Ruth Walker

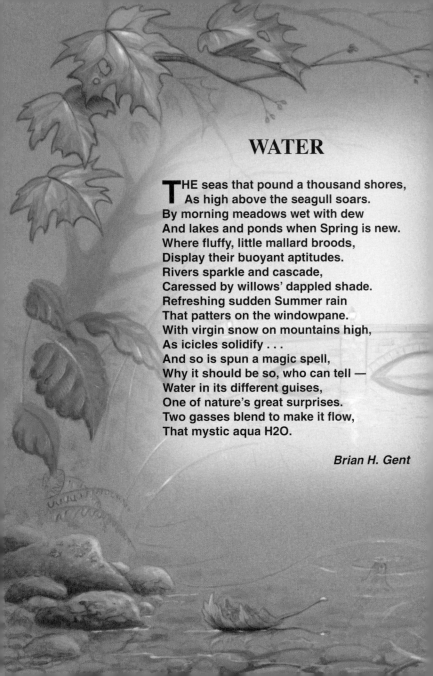

WATER

THE seas that pound a thousand shores,
As high above the seagull soars.
By morning meadows wet with dew
And lakes and ponds when Spring is new.
Where fluffy, little mallard broods,
Display their buoyant aptitudes.
Rivers sparkle and cascade,
Caressed by willows' dappled shade.
Refreshing sudden Summer rain
That patters on the windowpane.
With virgin snow on mountains high,
As icicles solidify . . .
And so is spun a magic spell,
Why it should be so, who can tell —
Water in its different guises,
One of nature's great surprises.
Two gasses blend to make it flow,
That mystic aqua H_2O.

Brian H. Gent

BEACH

SMOOTH as silk and soft as satin,
  rippled, damp, the new-washed sand,
dawn's high tide has left it shining,
cleansed of sign of human hand.

Soon the beach will pack with people,
noise and bustle fill the air,
ice-cream chimes and children squealing,
pop-song strains from distant fair.

Fish 'n' chips, and sweetie wrappers,
sandy skin and salt-splashed hair,
Dad digs holes and Mother paddles,
Grandma naps in picnic chair.

Slow the sun sinks gently seawards,
slow the day slides out of reach,
gentle waves reclaim the shoreline,
soft the rhythm of the beach.

Margaret Ingall

THE COLOURISTS

THEY came out here in the first years of the century,
Their eyes still drunk on Paris and Venice —
Here to the edge of the world, this blowing place,
Where the days are a constant gale,
Where everything is always changing
In a flurry of bright gusts.

They came out here
To put easels into the north wind and try to catch it,
To haul colours from sky and sea,
Tie them down to canvases — shreds of them,
Tattered edges — and take them back
In something that lasted forever.

Kenneth C. Steven

FOR TRAVEL WRITERS

I MAY not walk the ways again
 nor climb the hills that call me yet.
I can but dream of empty moors
where curlews cry and small streams fret
for tumbling larks and distant stars
are hidden now in clouded skies
and time has stolen from my step
the pebbled shores where sea-wrack lies.

But all of these that I have known,
the moors, the mountains and the shore,
with every page you give them back
and make me free of them once more.
So on my bookshelf now I keep
your words that show me once again
that every joy, each place I knew
in youth are mine and mine remain.

May Marshall

WHERE LILACS GROW

I LOVE to wander in the glade up near the pasture spring
through grasses wild and overhung with fragrant purple fringe,
in dappled shade suggestive of a richly perfumed wind,
where lilacs grow.

I cannot help but fill my arms with lush and heavy blooms
and dream away the sultriness of sleepy afternoons;
I'm loathe to leave the languor of this paradise too soon,
where lilacs grow.

Here, tall skies festooned with cloud kiss fields of velveteen
and in these gentle hours hedged with birch and evergreen,
a brief and tender glimpse of Heaven's glory can be seen,
where lilacs grow.

Rachel Wallace-Oberle

EVENING PAGEANT

DARK galleons drift through exotic seas,
 Riding, with sails full blown, the crimson deep.
The setting sun flames over purple trees,
To die in splendour as the shadows creep.

Thinly, above the sapphire sweep of hill,
A young moon glides in grace upon her way.
The amber glory fades, earth becomes still,
Twilight enfolds another drowsy day.

Joan Howes

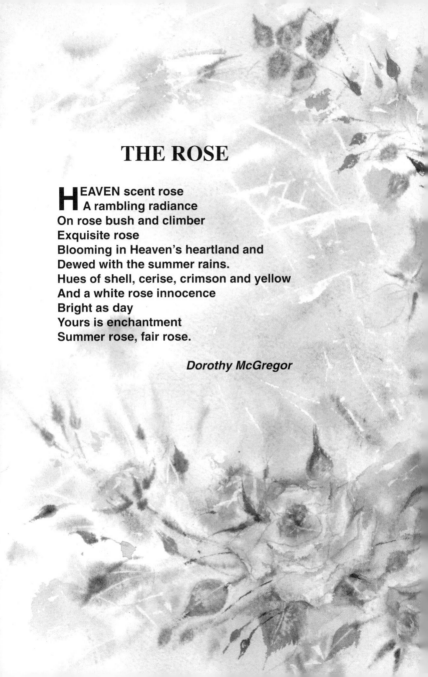

THE ROSE

HEAVEN scent rose
A rambling radiance
On rose bush and climber
Exquisite rose
Blooming in Heaven's heartland and
Dewed with the summer rains.
Hues of shell, cerise, crimson and yellow
And a white rose innocence
Bright as day
Yours is enchantment
Summer rose, fair rose.

Dorothy McGregor

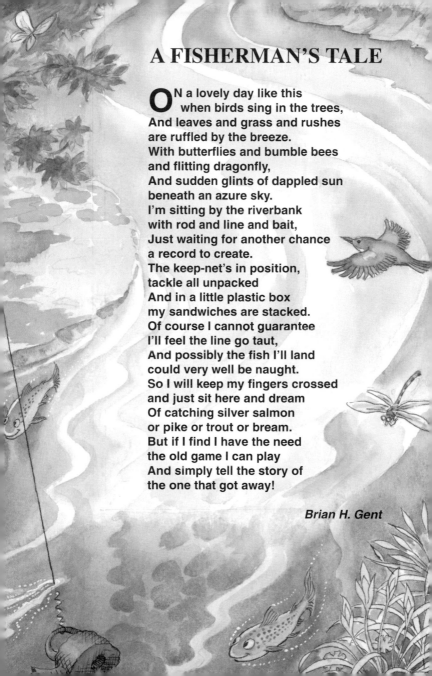

A FISHERMAN'S TALE

ON a lovely day like this
    when birds sing in the trees,
And leaves and grass and rushes
are ruffled by the breeze.
With butterflies and bumble bees
and flitting dragonfly,
And sudden glints of dappled sun
beneath an azure sky.
I'm sitting by the riverbank
with rod and line and bait,
Just waiting for another chance
a record to create.
The keep-net's in position,
tackle all unpacked
And in a little plastic box
my sandwiches are stacked.
Of course I cannot guarantee
I'll feel the line go taut,
And possibly the fish I'll land
could very well be naught.
So I will keep my fingers crossed
and just sit here and dream
Of catching silver salmon
or pike or trout or bream.
But if I find I have the need
the old game I can play
And simply tell the story of
the one that got away!

Brian H. Gent

THE EVENING TIDE

CLOUDS, beached upon the sky,
ripple in waves of dying light.
A pebble washed in pink, the moon,
skiffs the surface, playing
ducks and drakes with the dusk.

The high tide of darkness rolls in,
crashes over rooftops,
creating deep pools of shadow
where echoes swim;
its spray flecks the sky with stars
as daylight slowly ebbs.

Rowena M. Love

ROOTS

ON Gleniffer Braes
a kite with a pleated pigtail
bounced on an all blue sky,

and a whole landscape below,
a child ran backwards
with uncanny balance, chuckling

at his long awaited triumph.
Many more times in his life
he'd know the uncertain wind,

sometimes no wind at all. And he'd
recall his day on the hill,
the knowledge born of failure
and a persevering father.

Ian Nimmo White

SIMPLE THINGS

LEANING on a five-barred gate,
  The scene is set to ruminate.
A time to think of simple things,
Like butterflies with fairy wings.
Far distant hills and whisping clouds,
A world away from city crowds.
Dreamy brown-eyed Charolais,
While away the sunlit days.
A little lark sings, out of sight,
With magic scales of sheer delight.
Lambs that frisk in meadows lush,
By sapling, tree and burning bush.
From columbine and buttercup,
Bumble bees sweet nectar sup.
Such are the things that fascinate,
Just leaning on a five-barred gate.

Brian H. Gent

THE POOL

A FLICK of gold beneath the green,
    a quiver in the glass,
The water shifts and shivers while
it mirrors clouds that pass.
A goldfish glides through slender stems,
and slides past ferny frond,
The lily pads like sunshades spread
to hide the world beyond.
A secret realm, this fishy pool,
half-hid from human eye,
Yet by its side I love to sit
as Summer days slip by.

Margaret Ingall

MINIATURE PANSIES

LITTLE intimates I know
    your habit's not so much to grow,
but what in stature you may lack
a hundred-fold is given back
in the bright-fire of your glow.

Straining from your rockery bed
like keen spectators similarly scarfed,
each morning you delight the eye,
as week on week from early in July
you shout of purple, yellow, white and red.

It's your simplicity that's best,
for sure score-headed you might boast
there's none can outshine your appeal,
whose friendly faces make one feel
at once admired, admirer, guest and host.

John Ellis

THE LAST WORD

BENEATH my awning at the kitchen door,
I found a fragile miracle of sorts
Clinging to the brick, passed by before,
A hornets' nest.

Each hexagon is perfectly unique.
I watch although I dare not move or speak;
To irk this busy hamlet small and neat
Would not be best.

But crowds of yellow jackets everywhere,
Eyeing me at work with beady stares
Is really quite a worrisome affair,
I must confess.

Relinquished is my entrance at the side.
To those who now ferociously preside
With language often fierce and amplified,
I acquiesce.

Rachel Wallace-Oberle

THE END OF SUMMER

ROOTLING amongst the shrouded soil,
I snip at privet, tie back limp flowers,
let Solomon's seal spill its yellow.

Broom and rosemary yield to my shears;
fuchsia blooms still linger,
until hoar frost nips their fingers.

With heavy heads the sunflowers droop,
A single rose stands proud.
Beneath their glass, grapes turn musty,

tomatoes hang fire until they ripen
in the dark secret of a warm drawer.
Insects hum a golden waltz

as fires are lit in sleeping cottages
and smoke curls up from blackened chimneys.
Cutting through the raspberry canes,

my old hedgehog comes snuffling by
to make his nest among the leaves,
now that the nights are drawing in.

Ruth Walker

STATELY SORBUS

YOU gave us great pleasure
   stately sorbus,
from Spring's first
pricks of green
and creamy blossom,
to Autumn's flaming fantasy
and burnished berries.
Your feathered foliage,
a diurnal delight
in that drowsy,
dreamy Summer.

Don Robinson

AUBADE

EARLY morning, and the dew still moist upon the ground.
    An incandescent shimmer lambent on the cottage tile.
The cowman prods his field beasts from their lazy doze.
A blue-backed tractor gurgles and shudders on the field,
    its flat nose
purring into life, and clatters over the rough pile.
A pale sun shyly peeps above the mist-clad mound.
Sitting on a weather-vane a lone dove watches, caught
    by the spell
of new activity that had begun down on the meadow road.
Rising from the dung-mould heap a sharp smell
    stings the throat.
A windy gust gathers up the wild oat,
flies with it a while, then scatters all abroad.
Early workers meet and nod, remark upon the day,
and bob and bustle down the lane. Hidden in the hay,
stacked up in the barn loft, a field mouse preens
    its crumpled coat.

John Ellis

JEWEL BOX

ONE stride was all it took to cross
  The burn that splattered down the hill's steep curve,
But as my boot squelched down upon the sodden ground
I glimpsed, inset below, a bed of moss
That made me stop and turn again.
On that dark day the colours blazed and shone —
The russets and the ruby-garnet reds,
The saffron, amber, ochre, bronze —
Such colours as you see in toadstool wood
Or under coral seas. The day was still as dark,
But once again, an offered gift —
Beyond the price of choicest gems —
Had been accepted with a wondering gratitude.

Alice Elder

IMPRESSIVE MOON

IMPRESSIVE moon I see you there,
Enchantress in the cool night air,
Your countenance so full of grace
As if you rule your tranquil place;
And maybe on this night you do,
For no bright stars are peeping through.

The heaven's black, as black as tar,
Revealing just how great you are.
Even the wispy clouds that pass
Seem trivial against your mass,
As insignificant as I,
The watcher of the dark, night sky.

Alice Jean Don

THE PHANTOM

THE morning mist is silver,
The air is crisp and cold,
The sun is slowly rising
And turning grey to gold.
The landscape makes a picture
Becalmed within a frame.
Till comes a shift — a tremor
A hiss of gas and flame,
And there, beyond the treetops,
Like some phantasmal moon,
Upon the dawn comes riding
A giant air balloon.
Adrift upon an upstream,
If floats with cobweb grace,
Unhurried as the dawning,
At one with sky and space.
And far below, still dreaming
The sleeping village lies,
And no-one sees the voyager
That moves across the skies.

Margaret Ingall

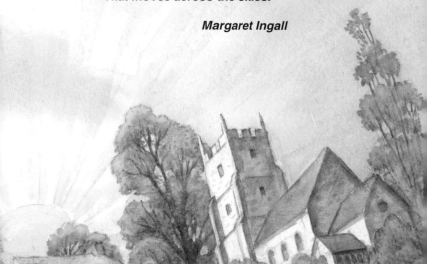

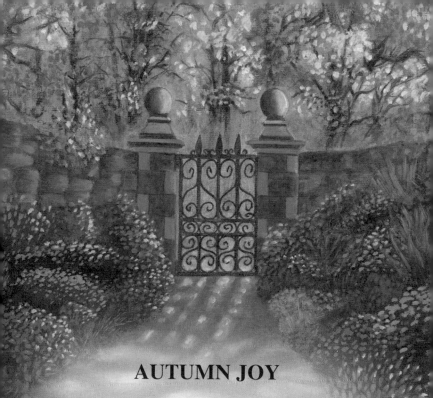

AUTUMN JOY

HAS there ever been a morning like this
   In October, when sun lips through trees kiss
weathered stone and paint the garden timber?
Has ever before seen such a miracle
of leaves, burnished both ochre and umber,
so languidly wrought beneath the garden wall?

Has such a bright furnace glow ever settled
quite so smilingly over grass metalled
with gold, to augur so peerless a day?
And was ever a prize so jostled for
in seasons' race won more deservedly,
than by this glorious morning in October?

John Ellis

MALLORY

ALL the long days rolling into years the snow fell softly
shrouding you in flakes of immortality.

Everest, mother goddess of mountains
welcomed, then held you
cradled in her white womb,
imprisoned you in an ice-cavern tomb.

You with your dreamer's eyes, did you reach
your goal? Stand as near the Heavens
as to touch a cloud drifting? Or did you fall
whirling through mist to die too soon?

When you closed your eyes, merging mind
into oblivion, did you hear the wind
rush, exulting in its destructive dance
through pinnacled chasms?

Did you picture the blinding beauty
of that white-peaked panorama
or the pink-flecked dawn? Did you know
the moon was tracing violet shadows on the snow?

Or did you remember the hills and forests you once knew,
the heather, moss and bracken, green and soft as velvet?

Catherine McArdle

CONKER

A TINY French polisher,
Invisible to our eyes,
Has been busy inside
The small green globe,
Building up layers
Of mahogany brown,
Deepening the hues
Hidden in grain,
Shining the masterpiece
For when — suddenly
Dropping from the bough —
The cushioned shell
Cracks open,
And reveals
To the cognoscente
At large
A miracle of art
Unmatched
By humankind.

David Elder

SAYING GOODBYE FOR THE LAST TIME

I KNEW it, from pantile to bedrock base
I knew this house, knew every spider's place.
Familiar walls, like a lover's flesh,
were studied for every mole and blemish.
I knew the rooms where conversation, play,
music, quietness, all made up the day.
I knew the corner where each holy hoard
of every child's miscellany was stored.

The kitchen's quirks, the bathroom's secret lore
of seismic vibrations beneath the floor.
I understood the spleen of irksome taps
that clocked away the night with vexing drips.
When tell-tale tiny mushrooms took my breath,
and wrinkled architrave spelled sudden death,
and boards bounced far too much, I knew the score
would always favour that destructive spore.

And yet, for all its perverse waywardness,
this house was home. I made it what it was
with drill and trowel and nail, but those who came
and filled it with their laughter made its name.
For best and worst, I loved it as it stood,
and leave it with regret and gratitude.

John Ellis

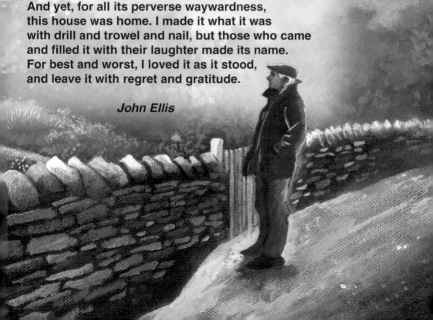

A WHISPER OF LEAVES

THE sound of the Autumn is soft as a sigh,
A whisper of leaves as a breeze passes by,
In colours bravura, both brilliant and bold,
She's clad in red-russet, in pumpkin and gold.
Her perfume's distinctive, of bonfire and smoke,
sharp as black leaf mould, and mellow as oak.
Her touch is of tree-bark, enduring and rough,
crisp as a corn stalk and conker-shell tough.
Her bounty is rich as the gown that she wears,
a tumble of berries, ripe apples and pears,
She pauses too briefly, then turning her face
abandons the world to the Winter's embrace.

Margaret Ingall

NOVEMBER PICTURES

THE city in November time
  Lies grey and dark and cold,
But in the woods and on the fells
There's russet, brown and gold.
Through city streets, the chill wind creeps,
But on our woodland walks
The wind goes sighing through the trees,
He whispers and he talks.
And higher on the climbing hills
He carries us along,
Then we are dancing with the clouds
And in our hearts a song.
The river running swift and sure,
The small streams racing by,
The heron standing, poised and still,
The wild birds flying high.

Through all the short, dark Winter days,
This beauty we'll remember,
The falling leaves, the hillside path,
The pictures of November.

Iris Hesselden

BENBECULA

AN island flattened to the wind;
  A flimsy thing in the Atlantic
Where colours come sudden
Out of the middle of everywhere.

When morning breaks each darkness
It turns more loch than land;
A moon of rocks and pools
As far as the eye can carry.

Those lochs lie in the land
Like watercolour lines.
Such a frail blue they're light,
Scuttering with the calls of birds.

A lark gracenotes the dawn,
Spinning notes from the sky,
Unravelling the tangle of clouds
That are ceaselessly blowing away.

I reach the rim of the sea, that's breathing in
  sudden hushes,
And I know what I have come to find
Is just as ever it was —
Always changing and still the same.

Kenneth C. Steven

SYMMETRY

TONIGHT I walked through snowy woods,
and for long moments stopped and stood
to contemplate a falling sky
of downy flakes that floated by,
and seemed to lift me from the earth,
above its gentle, sleeping curves.
One pointed star had pierced the dark
and bravely tried to play the part
of Heaven's canopy of light;
beyond the edges of the night
a frozen moon and starry show
winked out, surrendering to snow.
Within this hallowed interlude,
where man or beast did not intrude,
the woods and I both held our breath,
oblivious to cold or wet,
and humbled, witnessed silently
the spectacle of symmetry.

Rachel Wallace-Oberle

BRIDAL WHITE

THE snowflakes dancing down the breeze
  Come softly without sound,
And spread a fragile, feathered fleece
Upon the hardened ground.
A glistening mantle has been draped
On walls of old grey stone,
And gives to houses, roofs and eaves
A beauty of their own.

An ancient church, an old schoolhouse
Which stand on village green,
Are etched like pencilled silhouettes
Against the snowy scene.
All is transformed with silver wand
Waved by a Winter sprite,
Our old familiar world is dressed
In veil of bridal white.

Kathleen Gillum

The artists are:-

Matt Bain; Autumn Joy.
Jackie Cartwright; This Cold March Day, March Hares, Whispers In The Dark.
Henri Damoiseaux; Stately Sorbus.
John Dugan; Toads Crossing, For Travel Writers, A Fisherman's Tale, The Phantom.
Eunice Harvey; Paint A Poem, Jewel Box, Conker.
Harry McGregor; Spring, A Whisper Of Leaves.
Norma Maclean; Primroses, Country Woman, Rapture, The Colourists, Roots.
Keith Robson; My Little Friend, Grassland, Tranquillity, Country Church, Saying Goodbye For The Last Time.
Ruth M. L. Walker; Sequel, March Light, The Evening Tide.
Joseph Watson; February Wren, Awakening, Water.
Staff Artists; River Of Life, Teapots Line Your Stairs, Buried Treasure, Iona Ferry, Love In A Mist, Cat In Clover, Beach, Where Lilacs Grow, Evening Pageant, The Rose, Simple Things, The Pool, Miniature Pansies, The Last Word, The End Of Summer, Aubade, Impressive Moon, Mallory, November Pictures, Benbecula, Symmetry, Bridal White.